The Sea Power Library

BATTLESHIPS

The Sea Power Library

BATTLESHIPS

by Max Walmer

Rourke Publications, Inc.
Vero Beach, Florida 32964

This stunning view of the USS Wisconsin *truly reflects the enormous power and fighting capacity of battleships, the world's largest warships.*

Library of Congress Cataloging-in-Publication Data
Walmer, Max.
  Battleships.
  (The Sea power library)
  Includes index.
  Summary: Describes the history, types, weapons, and present uses of battleships, both in the United States and the Soviet Union.
  1. Battleships — Juvenile literature. [1. Battleships]
I. Title. II. Series.
V815.W35 1989   359.3'252   88-30696
ISBN 0-86625-083-2

Contents

Origins

At the start of World War Two (1939-1945), battleships were the very epitome of naval might and power. They were the largest and most powerful warships afloat. Unfortunately, many were sunk during the war, mostly by aircraft. By the end of the war, it was generally agreed that the day of the battleship was over. Many battleships remained in service until the early 1950s, but then they began to be laid up or put into storage. Finally, with the exception of one class, all were scrapped.

The four battleships of U.S. Navy's Iowa class were saved in case they might be needed in the future. It is no longer clear who that prudent man in the Pentagon was, but his foresight paid off. These battleships are now at sea again, playing a vital and much valued part in meeting the United States Navy's global commitment. Not only that, but after a gap of some 35 years since the previous battleship was built, the Soviet Union is now constructing a class of major warships which are, to all intents, battleships.

The battleship USS Missouri *passes under the Golden Gate bridge, escorted by a coastguard patrol boat, a tug spouting water, and a Sea King helicopter.*

Until World War Two battleships were the very essence of national power and prestige.

Throughout the sailing-ship era, there had always been large ships called men-of-war. In the nineteenth century, during the age of the iron-clad, very large ships emerged. These were known as **line-of-battle ships.** By the end of the century these had reached a **displacement** of some 12,000 tons and were armed with a variety of guns, the largest usually being of 11 to 12-inch **caliber.** At the start of the twentieth century the British, who at that time had the most powerful navy in the world, produced a revolutionary design. It was large, fairly fast, well protected with armor plating, and armed with ten 12-inch guns. It was known as the "all big-gun battleship," and ships of this type were called "dreadnoughts," after the name of the British ship. Like the U.S. Navy's nuclear submarine **USS** *Nautilus* in 1955, this British ship made all existing designs out-of-date. The world's major navies of the day (Germany, France, Russia, and the United States) were forced to follow suit and build dreadnoughts of their own.

During World War One (1914-1918) the battleship was the largest and most important ship at sea in any navy. It evolved into a fighting unit of unprecedented speed, size, and power. Between 1910 and 1920 displacements almost doubled, gun calibers and ranges improved almost beyond recognition, fire control and armored protection improved greatly, and propulsion systems became very efficient. The largest battleship fleets belonged to Great Britain and Imperial Germany, but these met only once, at the Battle of Jutland. That battle, on May 31, 1916, ended somewhat inconclusively, although the Germans did not seriously contest the mastery of the seas again.

Following the entry of the United States into the war on April 6, 1917, U.S. Navy battleships served in the Atlantic and also joined the British Grand Fleet facing the Imperial German Navy in the North Sea. The most up-to-date U.S. battleships in World War One were those of the New Mexico class, which consisted of three ships, completed just as the war ended. These battleships had a displacement of 33,000 tons, mounted twelve 14-inch guns, 14-inch armored protection, and were the first major ships to be fitted with turbo-electric drive.

Crew members man the rail as the battleship USS Missouri leaves the dock en route to re-commissioning in San Francisco.

Commander of the sixth fleet, Vice Admiral Moranville watches the USS Saratoga aircraft carrier from the bridge of the USS Iowa.

An aerial view of a battle group in formation, led by the battleship USS Missouri.

By the time of her entry into World War Two the United States had a large force of battleships. This force was split into two fleets, one facing the German threat in the Atlantic and the other the Japanese threat in the Pacific. The latest battleships to enter U.S. Navy service in 1941 were the four ships of the South Dakota class; these displaced 44,519 tons, were armed with nine 16-inch guns, and had a maximum speed of 27 **knots.** After very successful war service all four were decommissioned in the 1960s. Two were later scrapped, but two — *Massachusetts* and *Alabama* — are preserved as memorials in their name states.

U.S. entry to the war was the direct result of the Japanese attack on the United States' Pacific Fleet at Pearl Harbor on December 7, 1941. Of eight battleships present, three were sunk, one capsized, and the remaining four seriously damaged.

A Californian welcome for the USS Missouri as she heads into San Francisco Bay.

Flanked by the USS Dewy *guided-missile destroyer and the USS* Ticonderoga, *the USS* Iowa *steams into the morning sun.*

Battleships played a significant part in World War Two naval operations, although as the war progressed it became increasingly obvious that the aircraft carrier was more important than the battleship. Numerous engagements in the Pacific included the last battleship-versus-battleship action at the Battle of Surigao Strait on October 24 and 25, 1944. A Japanese **task force,** centered upon two battleships, attempted to disrupt U.S. landings on the Philippine island of Leyte. They were met by a U.S. group, including six battleships, commanded by Rear Admiral J. B. Oldendorf. In a fierce battle the Japanese force was totally defeated, with both battleships, a cruiser, and four destroyers sunk. The final rounds of the battle were fired by the battleship USS *West Virginia,* which had been sunk in the Japanese attack on Pearl Harbor almost three years before. She had been raised and rebuilt, and now she was having her revenge.

USS New Jersey *cruises gracefully through the Panama Canal.*

The four geared turbines that drive each Iowa-class battleship carry four shafts, each of which has an enormous screw.

During World War Two some very fine battleship designs were produced. The German *Bismarck,* for example, was so well designed that it took most of the British navy to sink her when she roamed the Atlantic for a brief period in May 1941. The Imperial Japanese Navy produced the two ships of the Yamato class; these huge warships each displaced 71,659 tons and were armed with nine 18-inch guns, the largest and most heavily armed battleships ever built. Both were sunk by carrier-based torpedo bombers of the U.S. Navy: *Musashi* on October 24, 1944, and *Yamato* on April 7, 1945.

The British and French had also developed two good battleship designs during the war. With a displacement of 47,500 tons, the French Richelieu class were as large as the United States' South Dakotas. Their main armament of eight 15-inch guns was mounted in two four-gun turrets, both positioned forward of the bridge superstructure. This placement was relatively unusual; it was more common for at least one of the big gun turrets to be sited aft of the superstructure, at the rear end of the ship. The final

The power of the battleship is used not only against other warships but also against targets on land.

British battleship was **HMS** *Vanguard,* armed with eight 15-inch guns and displacing 51,450 tons; completed in April 1946, she was too late to see service in the war.

After the war, older battleships were scrapped almost immediately, and only a few of the most modern served on for a few more years. By 1950 the British, who had once had the largest fleet of battleships in the world, had only the *Vanguard* left in service; she was decommissioned in 1955 and scrapped in 1960. The French Richelieu-class battleships remained in service somewhat longer, even serving off Indo-China during the French war there (1947-1954) and taking part in the Suez operations in 1956. Both were finally scrapped in 1968 and 1969. Most U.S. battleships were decommissioned in the 1940s and 1950s and were scrapped in the 1960s. The sole exception was the Iowa class, the last and finest of American "battlewagons," for whom a different future was planned.

The guns of the USS Missouri *are capable of throwing shells a distance of more than 20 miles.*

The enormous deck area of the USS New Jersey *is seen to good effect in this picture.*

Iowa Class

The origin of the Iowa-class design can be traced back to the early 1930s when the U.S. Navy was seeking a well-armed, well-armored battleship that would be able to operate with fast aircraft carrier task groups. This meant that the ship needed to be able to operate at speeds of up to 33 knots, which, in turn, required a power plant capable of delivering 200,000 shaft horsepower. Six ships were ordered altogether.

USS Missouri *is one of four Iowa-class battleships laid down between June 1940 and January 1941.* ▶

Bottom Right

The Iowa-class battleships were launched in 1942 and 1943, within a year of the Japanese attack on Pearl Harbor.

Iowa -Class Ships

Name	Number	Ordered	Launched	Commissioned
Iowa	BB-61	1938	August 27, 1942	February 22, 1943
New Jersey	BB-62	1938	December 7, 1942	May 23, 1943
Missouri	BB-63	1939	January 29, 1944	June 11, 1944
Wisconsin	BB-64	1939	April 16, 1943	April 16, 1944
Illinois	BB-65	1940	Canceled 1945	Scrapped 1945
Kentucky	BB-66	1940	Canceled 1947	Scrapped 1959

As first built, the Iowas were armed with nine 16-inch guns mounted in three triple turrets, two forward and one aft. As secondary armament, twenty 5-inch dual-purpose (**DP**) guns were housed in ten twin turrets, five on either side of the main superstructure. Anti-aircraft (**AA**) armament varied between individual ships, ranging from 60 to 80 40mm guns and 50 to 60 20mm cannon. The crew totaled 1,921 officers and enlisted men. With a main belt 12.25 inches thick, the Iowa-class battleships had excellent armored protection. Earlier battleships had not been too well protected against plunging shells and bombs. A remarkable feature of the Iowa class was the provision of two heavily armored decks of 4.7 inches and 5.5 inches thickness respectively, with a splinter deck of 1.5 inches between them, giving a total thickness of 11.7 inches. The large, open fantail gave plenty of space for two airplane catapults. The three Vought OS2U Kingfisher scout airplanes were accommodated below deck in a spacious hangar.

Iowa entered service in August 1943, and for the first two months of her service life she patrolled in the North Atlantic off Newfoundland. The U.S. was anticipating a possible breakout by the German battleship *Tirpitz*, at that time sheltering in a Norwegian fjord. In January 1944 *Iowa* moved to the

The primary armament of these enormous battleships comprises nine 16-inch guns and twelve 5-inch guns.

Pacific and joined the recently completed *New Jersey* in accompanying fast carrier forces in the campaign against the Japanese-held islands. Both took part in the Battles of the Philippine Sea and of Leyte Gulf. *Missouri* and *Wisconsin* entered service in late 1944; they were present at the landings on Iwo Jima and Okinawa and accompanied the fast carrier task groups in the final raids on Japan. *Missouri* was slightly damaged by a Japanese kamikaze (suicide) attack off Okinawa. The damage was quickly repaired, and *Missouri* had the distinction of being selected for the signature of the Japanese surrender document on September 2, 1945. The last two ships of the class, *Illinois* and *Kentucky,* had not been completed when World War Two ended. After some indecision, they were both scrapped.

With eight boilers and four geared turbines, each Iowa-class ship is capable of a maximum speed of approximately 35 knots.

Each 16-inch gun can fire a 2,700-pound shell a maximum range of 23 miles.

War At Sea

Tugs gently nudge the USS New Jersey toward her berth.

The four Iowa-class ships that had seen duty were placed in reserve in the late 1940s but were reactivated for the Korean War. Each undertook one six-month deployment, except for *Missouri,* which took two. *Missouri*'s first deployment was from September 1950 to March 1951 and her second from October 1952 to March 1953. *New Jersey* was the second ship deployed in the area from May to November 1951. *Wisconsin* took up her tour of duty in November 1951, handing over to *Iowa* for her deployment from April to October 1952.

Their tasks were to provide fire support for the armies ashore and to act as task-force **flagships.**

They fired many rounds against ground targets during this period but did not themselves come under attack. *Wisconsin* collided with a destroyer in 1956, and her bow was so damaged that it was removed and replaced by the bow of the *Kentucky,* on which work had been suspended in 1947. In 1958 all four battleships were back in reserve.

At the height of the Vietnam War in 1968 there was once again a need for sea-based fire support for the army troops ashore. *New Jersey* was brought out of reserve and recommissioned. Her equipment was sadly out-of-date, and all her AA armament had been removed, but nevertheless she was given only a minor update before being sent to Vietnamese waters. During her entire World War Two career, *New Jersey* had fired only 771 shells from her 16-inch guns, but during her brief tour of duty off Vietnam she fired no less than 5,688! She was preparing for a second tour off Vietnam in late 1969 when she was ordered back into reserve.

In 1973, the four Iowa-class battleships were almost scrapped. A brief awakening of interest in the battleships convinced the U.S. Navy to keep them for a while longer. This was very fortunate, because soon after, in the mid-1970s, intelligence began to reach the West about the new Soviet 25,000-ton battlecruisers of the Kirov class, then being built. The U.S. had no need to build new ships to match the Kirov class. The four Iowa-class battleships were still in reserve, and their hulls were in excellent condition.

Consequently, it was proposed in 1975 to form missile-armed surface action groups centered on the battleships to operate in low-threat areas where a carrier-based group was not justified. After a great deal of discussion, President Reagan authorized the modernization of *New Jersey* in 1981 at a cost of $326 million: $170 million for repairs and refurbishment, and the remainder for new weapons systems and updated electronics.

Sailors man the railings and gun turrets, as USS Iowa *heads for the open sea.*

Iowa-class battleships are protected with armor up to 12 inches thick.

USS New Jersey *shows off her enormous bulk in this dry-dock view.*

New Jersey rejoined the fleet on December 28, 1982, followed by *Iowa* on April 28, 1984, and *Missouri* on May 10, 1986. There was some doubt as to whether *Wisconsin* would also be brought out of reserve, but the go-ahead was finally given and she

Carrying a total crew of more than 2,000 officers and men, each ship is like a floating town, and must be supplied with extensive stocks of ammunition and stores.

Last of the Iowa class to be re-introduced into service,
USS Wisconsin *is seen here during her re-fit program.*

was the last to be recommissioned in January 1989. In 1983 *New Jersey* deployed with the U.S. Sixth Fleet in the Mediterranean, where she provided heavy fire support for the U.S. Marine Corp force stationed in Beirut.

The reactivation of these ships is a triumph, and it has been achieved at a cost for each ship of less than that for a new frigate of the Oliver Hazard Perry class, the navy's "economy" class. The U.S. Navy owes a large debt of gratitude to the man who decided to preserve these fine ships instead of scrapping them, as was done in every other navy. The British Royal Navy, for instance, could well regret the passing of HMS *Vanguard,* the finest British battleship, completed in 1946 and scrapped in 1960.

Weapons

Part of the superstructure with secondary armament and the bridge area are clearly seen in this port shot of the USS Missouri.

◄ *Helicopters routinely move between the Iowa-class battleships and other surface vessels in the fleet.*

The main armament of today's Iowa-class battleships remains the massive 16-inch guns, which are capable of firing armor-piercing projectiles as far away as 23 miles at a theoretical rate of 2 rounds per gun per minute. Each shell weighs just over one ton, while each three-gun turret weighs an additional 1,700 tons and requires 77 men in the mount as well as about 30 more in the magazine. Production of the barrels and ammunition has long since ended, but no less than

In addition to large and very powerful guns, the Iowa-class ships carry a wide range of short-, medium-, and long-range missiles.

The total armament of the Iowa-class battleships is eight 4-missile Tomahawk SSM launchers, eight 4-missile Harpoon SSM launchers, nine 16-inch guns in three triple turrets, twelve 5-inch guns, and four 20mm Mark 15 Phalanx CIWS. The ships also carry four **LAMPS** II or III helicopters.

Secondary guns open up during target practice.

Action Groups

How will the mighty Iowa-class battleships be used in the 1990s? First, it is important to appreciate that they would never deploy on their own, but always as the central element in a surface action group. Although the battleships have excellent anti-surface weapons, being armed with both guns and missiles, they are not capable of looking after themselves against every threat in a modern combat environment. They have a good short-range air defense capability, but they do not have the highly specialized radars to detect aircraft at long ranges, nor do they have the weapons to use against aerial targets so far away. They need escorts with such a capability. The battleships also lack an effective anti-submarine capability of their own. Thus they also need an escort of **ASW** destroyers and frigates. All these warships in the surface action group will need supplies and fuel, which necessitate what the navy terms "underway replenishment," in other words, one or more oilers and supply ships.

Battleships are vital to combined naval and marine operations; they can be used to bombard shore targets prior to beach landings.

USS Iowa moves through the Panama Canal.

The United States Navy plans to have four surface action groups should a war take place, each group centered upon an Iowa-class battleship. Two of these groups would be in direct support of **NATO**: one in the Mediterranean and the second in the Atlantic. The third group would be in the Indian Ocean/Persian Gulf area, and the fourth in the Western Pacific. The most powerful of the escorts are two cruisers, almost certainly Ticonderoga-class ships. They combine a powerful air-defense weapons fit of Standard surface-to-air missiles (**SAM**) with the Aegis weapons system for detection of hostile threats and command-and-control of the subsequent engagements.

There would then be four destroyers, probably of the Spruance class, which combine good medium-range air defenses (Sea Sparrow SAMs) with a strong anti-submarine warfare capability. Then there would be four frigates, probably of the Oliver Hazard Perry class, whose primary role is anti-submarine warfare.

Finally, the surface action group would be accompanied by its own replenishment ships. These are very large, specially designed vessels, which

The sleek outline of the Iowa-class battleship is seen to good effect here in this sunset view.

carry fuel, ammunition, food, stores, and spares. They enable the warships to stay at sea for log periods without having to return to port. They replenish the warships while still traveling at normal speed by maneuvering until they are close together; lines and hoses are then passed from one ship to another and the warship's requirements are transferred. The latest U.S. Navy replenishment oilers of the Kaiser class, for example, can carry 86,400 barrels of fuel oil for ships' engines, 54,000 barrels of fuel for aircraft engines (there will be many helicopters in the group), 390 tons of drinking water, 327 tons of feed water, plus a large tonnage of dry stores (food, spare parts, and so on). Such a ship is, in effect, a floating warehouse and gas station, and the warships could not survive for long without its assistance.

Battleships are a powerful means of demonstrating commitment to treaties and international agreements.

Few nations can afford the luxury of battleships, but they are undoubtedly the supreme expression of power and national prestige.

Battle groups at sea involve many different types of ships, including cruisers, destroyers, and frigates. ▶

Once at sea, such a surface action group, commanded by an admiral, has to protect itself against several sources of attack. The escorts position themselves to create a protective screen around the battleship. Spacing between the ships is determined by two main factors: the range and capability of their weapons systems and sensors and the likelihood of nuclear attack. The first factor tends to draw the ships closer together to link the effective areas of their systems, while the second tends to make them move farther apart so that too many ships cannot be lost to one nuclear weapon. The group commander's task is to strike the right balance. Ships are allocated sectors to patrol and are given freedom to move within these areas as they advance along the general axis towards the group's destination.

Although the surface action group may not include its own aircraft carrier, the group would seldom, if ever, move outside the cover of friendly aircraft, either carrier- or land-based. This is because aircraft attack is a prime threat to warships, as was proved during World War Two and again during the British action to recover the Falkland Islands from Argentina in 1982.

The main weapons of the battleships are their nine 16-inch guns, which could be used either to attack enemy ships or, and this is the more likely, to bombard targets ashore. Bombarding targets ashore normally requires forward observers, specially trained officers positioned so that they can see the target and "spot" the fall of the rounds. They then pass back corrections by radio to the ship, so that the guns' point of aim can be adjusted to bring the rounds right down on the target. Such forward observers could be either ashore, in a helicopter, or in an aircraft. These bombardments are extremely accurate and if all guns fire together at the same target (known as a "broadside") they deliver nine 1.2-ton shells — a total of 10.85 tons arriving simultaneously! — out to a maximum range of 18 miles.

USS Iowa *fires her 16-inch guns while carrier USS* ▶ **Saratoga** *is refueling in the background.*

Bottom Right
Raised for firing, each gun is then lowered immediately for re-loading.

The USS Iowa *demonstrates the fire power of her big guns to guests during a visit to Central America in February 1987.*
▼

Kirov Class

Over the years, the Soviet navy possessed a few battleships but only one class of true dreadnoughts: three ships of the Gangut class. Built between 1909 and 1914, they were all scrapped in the 1950s. For many years the largest surface warships in the Soviet navy were the 14 ships in the Sverdlov class. Of 17,200 tons displacement, they were built between 1951 and 1956. The Soviet destroyer and cruiser construction program during the 1960s and 1970s showed a gradual increase in size, culminating in the 12,000-ton Slava class. Nevertheless, Western experts were taken by surprise when news began to reach them of a new class of very large ships under construction: the largest warships, other than aircraft carriers, to be built since the completion of the British HMS *Vanguard* in August 1946.

First introduced in 1980, the Soviet battleship Kirov *was followed by the* Frunze *in 1983, and two more are known to be nearing completion.*

This new Soviet class is named after the first ship, *Kirov,* and is classified by the Soviet navy as *Atomny Raketny Kreyser* (nuclear-powered, missile-armed cruiser). In the West, these ships are usually called battlecruisers after a type of large, heavily armed and fast but lightly armored ship. The *Kirov* was laid down in 1973, launched in 1977, and commissioned in 1980. The second of the class, *Frunze,* joined the fleet in 1984. One more ship of this class is fitting out, and a fourth is under construction; these will almost certainly include further refinements of the weapons and sensor fits. There is no further information on the Soviet navy's plans beyond that. We can assume that having discovered the value of such large ships in peacetime power projection (to say nothing of their value in war), they will continue to build additional warships, perhaps even larger.

The Kirov *is the Soviet Union's first nuclear-powered surface warship and has an estimated top speed of 33 knots, combined with a range of 14,000 miles.*

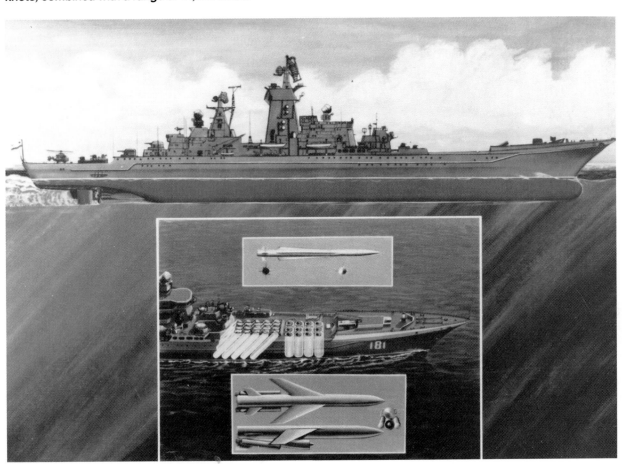

Armament

The main armament of all earlier battleships and battlecruisers was the "big gun." The ultra-modern Kirov class, however, has a powerful battery of twenty long-range **SS-N**-19 surface-to-surface missile launchers, housed in a multi-cell vertical-launch battery (probably armored) located in the forecastle. These missiles have a range of some 300 nautical miles. Over-the-horizon targeting data is supplied in three ways: by a command post ashore (which passes the data to the missile via a communications satellite), direct by surveillance satellites using electronic intelligence, active radar, and infra-red detection techniques, or by on-board helicopters. The Kirovs carry three Kamov Ka-25 Hormone or Kamov Ka-27 Helix helicopters.

The Kirov-class battlecruisers have sophisticated air-defense systems. The **SA-N**-6 SAM is a high-performance surface-to-air missile system, using track-via-missile guidance, which enables the ship to engage several targets simultaneously. The missile itself has a range in excess of 46.5 nautical miles with a very high speed of Mach 5 to 6, five to six times the speed of sound. The twelve launchers are each supplied by a rotating eight-round magazine.

*The **Kirov** guided-missile cruiser has barely adequate fire power from its guns, but carries a large number of surface-to-surface and surface-to-air missiles.*

The short-range SAM systems differ between the two ships. In the *Kirov* the primary short-range SAM is SA-N-4, a "pop up" launcher housed in a magazine bin containing 18 to 20 missiles. In *Frunze,* however, these are supplemented by the SA-N-9. In the *Kirov* all air-defense missile launchers were on the forecastle, leaving the aft quadrant somewhat unprotected; this has been overcome in the *Frunze* by positioning two four-tube SA-N-8 launchers on the fantail, displacing the 30mm gatling CIWS, which have been moved to the aft superstructure. *Kirov* mounts two dual-purpose 3.9-inch guns aft. In *Frunze* these have been replaced by one twin 5.1-inch turret, identical to those fitted to the Sovremenny- and Slava-class cruisers. Close-range anti-missile defense in both ships relies on four groups of two 30mm gatling guns, located in the four "corners" of the ship to give all around coverage.

These Soviet ships have to a play a major part in their own anti-submarine defense, although there would, of course, be an escort of destroyers or frigates. *Kirov* has a reloadable launcher for SS-N-14 ASW missiles on the forecastle, but this has been omitted on *Frunze*. Both ships have rocket launchers, torpedo tubes, and three Kamov Ka-25

Soviet ships of the Kirov class are part of an integrated naval force involving a wide range of ocean-going ships.

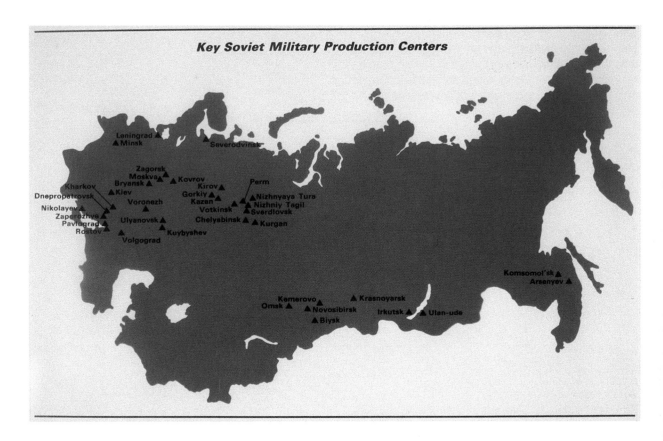

Key Soviet Military Production Centers

Leningrad
Minsk
Severodvinsk
Zagorsk
Moskva
Bryansk
Kovrov
Kirov
Perm
Kharkov
Kiev
Gorkiy
Nizhnyaya Tura
Dnepropetrovsk
Kazan
Nizhniy Tagil
Voronezh
Votkinsk
Sverdlovsk
Nikolayev
Chelyabinsk
Kurgan
Zaporozhye
Ulyanovsk
Pavlograd
Rostov
Kuybyshev
Volgograd
Komsomol'sk
Arsenyev
Kemerovo
Krasnoyarsk
Omsk
Novosibirsk
Irkutsk
Ulan-ude
Biysk

Hormone-A/B (or Ka-27 Helix) helicopters for ASW and missiles guidance.

Modern warships depend upon electronic devices to find the enemy, to guide missiles, and for navigation. Soviet navy ships are well known for their extensive electronics equipment, evidence of which is provided by the large number of antennas. The Kirov class is particularly well equipped.

To detect submarines, there is a large low-frequency sonar in the bow and low-frequency variable-depth sonar (**VDS**) in the stern. The extensive electronics suite includes two major three-dimensional air surveillance radars, nicknamed "Top Pair" and "Top Steer," plus individual gun and missile fire control radars. *Kirov* is fitted with the standard 1970s **ECM/ESM** outfit, with eight Side Globe broad-band jammers and four Rum Tub ESM antennas around the top of the tower mast. Neither of these is fitted in *Frunze,* each being replaced by a different type of bell-shaped **radome.** The communications fit is also changed in the newer ship. The main visible change is the replacement of *Kirov's* Vee-Tube C by large bell-covered satellite antennas.

This map of Soviet military production centers, with their concentrated grouping toward the northwest portion of the U.S.S.R., also shows the northern location of the Leningrad shipyards, which are frequently ice-bound in winter.

This appears to represent a logical change in emphasis from long-distance high-frequency communications, notoriously vulnerable to interception and jamming, to satellite links, which are more secure and able to handle much greater traffic volumes.

The total armament of the two Kirov-class ships includes:

	Kirov	Frunze
Missile launchers	Twenty SS-N-19 (20)	Twenty SS-N-19 (20)
(Number of missiles):	Twelve SA-N-6 (96)	Twelve SA-N-6 (96)
	Two twin SA-N-4 (40)	Two twin SA-N-4 (40)
		Sixteen SA-N-9 (128)
Guns:	Two single 100mm	One twin 130mm
	Eight 30mm CIWS	Eight 30mm CIWS
Anti-submarine weapons:	One twin SS-N-14	—
	One 12-barrel RBU-6000 mortar	One 12-barrel RBU-6000 mortar
	Two 6-barrel RBU-1000 mortars	Two 6-barrel RBU-1000 mortars
Torpedo tubes:	Two quintuple (2×5) 21-inch (533mm) torpedo tubes	Two quintuple (2×5) 21-inch (533mm) torpedo tubes

Soviet naval forces use special communications and radar-tracking ships to link by satellite the many ships operating in international waters. ▲

Soviet warships bristle with missile launch tubes but are frequently under-gunned. ▶

The guided-missile cruiser, like this Slava-class vessel, ◄ is another type of large warship operated by the Soviet Union.

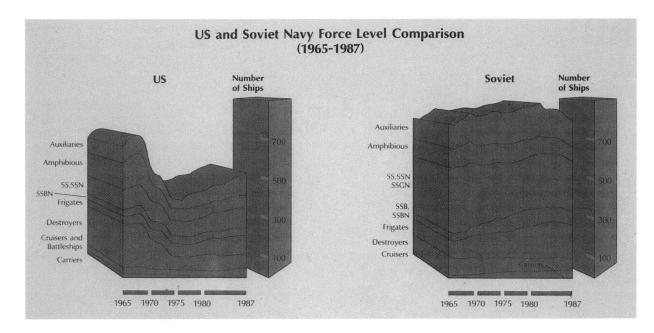

US and Soviet Navy Force Level Comparison
(1965-1987)

The relative strength of U.S. and Soviet naval programs can be seen in this chart, which shows the number of ships in service with each of the two navies.

It is difficult to compare the U.S. Navy's Iowa-class battleships with the Soviet navy's Kirov-class battle-cruisers. The Iowas were designed in the late 1930s, and they have proved to be very adaptable and durable. If today an American naval architect was given a blank sheet of paper and instructed to design a modern gun/missile ship, he would probably come up with something more like the Kirov than the Iowa. The Iowas' propulsion systems are old, and being non-nuclear their range is not nearly as great as that of the Soviet ships. Also, their heavy armor is much thicker than would be needed today, although it would be very difficult for a modern missile warhead to penetrate. The guns confer a capability on the Iowas that the Kirovs lack, but the manpower required — some 100 men per turret — is enormous. Despite these deficiencies, the Iowa class fulfills a requirement met by no other ship.

◄ *Increasing interest in global activity has caused the Soviets to develop small carriers for vertical-launched aircraft and helicopters, complementing their battle cruisers.*

Abbreviations

AA	Anti-Aircraft
ASW	Anti-Submarine Warfare
CIWS	Close-In Weapons System
	A multi-barreled gun with a very high rate of fire for "last-ditch" protection, especially against missiles.
DP	Dual Purpose
ECM/ESM	Electronic Counter-Measures/Electronic Support Measures
HMS	Her Majesty's Ship
	Designation for warships of the British Royal Navy, such as HMS *Invincible*.
LAMPS	Light Airborne Multi-Purpose System
	U.S. Navy helicopter-borne ASW system. The two LAMPS helicopters in service are LAMPS-I, the Kamen SH-2F Seasprite, and LAMPS-II, The Sikorsky SH-60B Seahawk.
NATO	North Atlantic Treaty Organization
RBU-	Designation for Soviet Navy ASW mortars. It is always followed by a number, such as RBU-6000, which indicates the range in meters.
SAM	Surface-to-Air Missile
SA-N-	Surface-to-Air — Navy
	U.S. Navy designator for Soviet SAM systems deployed on board warships. Always followed by a type number such as SA-N-4.
SSM	Surface-to-Surface Missile
SS-N-	Surface-to-Surface — Navy
	U.S. Navy designator for Soviet SSM systems deployed on boats and warships. Always followed by a type number, such as SS-N-2.
USS	United States Ship
	Designation for a warship of the United States Navy such as USS *Bronstein*.
VDS	Variable Depth Sonar

Glossary

Caliber

The diameter of a gun barrel, measured in inches or millimeters. The length of the barrel is also usually expressed in multiples of the caliber. Thus, the *Iowa's* 16-inch/50 guns have a length of 50 x 16 = 800 inches.

Displacement

The measure of the size of a ship, given by the amount of water it displaces. Figures given in this book are for "full-load displacement," when the ship is fully armed, equipped, and loaded for war.

Flagship

The ship in a task group that holds the commanding admiral's headquarters. It flies his flag to indicate this role.

Knot

The measure of speed at sea.
1 knot = 1 nautical mile per hour.

Line-of-battle ships

Major warships in the sailing era, which took their place "in the line" when engaging the enemy fleet, which would also be in line. Frigates were considered too lightly armed to take their place in the line. The term was eventually shortened to "battleships," meaning the heaviest, gun-armed warships.

Nautical mile

1 nautical mile = 1.1515 statute miles
= 6,082 feet

Radome

A bulbous dome designed to cover the antenna of a radar transmitter.

Task force

A tactical grouping of warships, assembled to carry out a particular task.

Variable Depth Sonar

A device for detecting submarines. It consists of a streamlined body containing hydrophones, that is lowered on a long cable from the fantail of a warship. Its depth is varied to match the underwater conditions.

Index

Page references in *italics* indicate photographs or illustrations.